EARTH GIANT TREE GIFT SERIES – BOOK 1

Oak Tree's Gift

ROCHELLE HEVEREN

 TREE VOICE PUBLISHING

Earth Giant Tree Gift Series: Oak Tree's Gift

TREE VOICE PUBLISHING PTY LTD
ACN. 627 784 294 ABN . 94627784294
4 Wirreanda Court Blackburn Victoria 3130 AUSTRALIA
Phone +613 9878 4600
Email: hello@treevoice.global
www.treevoice.global

First published in 2018
Copyright text © Rochelle Heveren
Copyright © Tree Voice Publishing

business.facebook.com/TreeVoiceAuthor
www.facebook.com/RochelleHeverenAuthor
Instagram: @rochelle_with_love_x

All rights reserved. No part of this publication may be reproduced in whole or in part, stored in a retrievable system, or transmitted in any form or by any means, electronic, mechanical, photocopying, recording or otherwise, without written permission of the copyright holder or publisher.

Designed by Tree Voice Publishing Pty Ltd
Printed by Ingram Spark
ISBN: 978-0-6483521-0-5 (paperback)

 A catalogue record for this book is available from the National Library of Australia

Praise for 'Oak Tree's Gift'

"Soul magician Rochelle has a beautiful conversation with the huge Oak Tree that grows beside her farmhouse. While reading her gentle words, I actually felt the resounding wisdom in this unique relationship. The gift that makes 'Oak Tree's Gift' book so special."

Nancy Mills
The Spirited Woman

"The ancient mystical wisdom that pours from the Tree is both life giving and life changing! Having someone such as Rochelle to open her heart to this wisdom, and then share it with the world is a precious gift beyond measure. In her book 'Oak Tree's Gift', Rochelle brings to us incredible life lessons that have the ability to transform our lives in amazing ways. A beautiful book written from Oak's heart to the hearts of those ready to hear! Thank you Rochelle for creating the time and the space to pen your conversations so we can all benefit from this magical little book."

Dr Geraldine Teggelove, Msc
International Best Selling Author

"Rochelle is deeply gifted in the working realms of nature, particularly trees. Her unique understanding of their expressions is captivating. Equally, the words of the majestic Oak speaks to us in such a way that allows for our own growth to emerge. Wise and boundless, the soul of Oak imbues universal truth through the art of story – worth listening to with every fibre of your being. There is so much we can learn from her. Thank you Rochelle for this gift."

Deanne Mathews
self-love-woman

Foreword

Oak Tree's Gift is the channelled teachings of one of Earth's great Grand Mothers. The wise hundred-year-old Oak brings you truth, boundaries and a unique way of guiding life's journey.

She'll remind you of the importance of holding space, the beauty of a bird's balance, your reflection in others, gifts and the importance of support. She'll guide you through the challenges of self-sabotage, judgement, feeling confused and being full of worry. She will help open your heart and mind to untold possibilities and assist you to live your highest truth with compassion, stillness and unique balance.

Being supported with the magic of *Oak Tree's Gift* is like resting your back her trunk and listening to her whispers of great wisdom. Allow her words to caress you with love.

This inspiring gift book is designed to unlock your own heart's wisdom. Rochelle invites you to discover the magic love and support that she experienced, sitting and resting her back against the Oak Tree.

Written in North East Victoria, Australia

Contents

Introduction 1

Chapter 1: Yesterday's Story 3

Chapter 2: Death of the Soul 8

Chapter 3: Holding Space 14

Chapter 4: Birds' Balance 18

Chapter 5: Support 24

Chapter 6: Reflections 28

Chapter 7: Togetherness 31

Chapter 8: Self-Sabotage 34

Chapter 9: War's Battle Never Won 40

Chapter 10: Oak's Gift 44

Chapter 11: Celebration 48

Introduction

I walk with light feet towards the massive oak tree standing beside my farmhouse. The sudden burst of recent summer sun has heated and dried the earth. Dust puffs where I tread.

My beautiful oak stands, tall and solid. I know her, yet I have never sat at her base in more than 15 years of living beside her. Now, my back rests against her thick trunk. Bark covers her like wrinkles, deep crevices of wisdom, revealing more than her hundred plus years.

I remember back to a time before my physical eyes drank in her grand presence. I'd seen her in a vision. In meditation, I had been shown this very oak tree, journeying through all the seasons of her year. Shedding leaves in autumn ... standing bare in winter ... new buds forming in spring ... birthing fresh leaves in summer. A wide canopy, providing shade and beauty. Before I met her physically, she was already calling my name.

Back in late 2001, I was driving with my young family through the country. We had longed for a place where the boys could ride motorbikes and run free. We discovered a farm property, though it wasn't for sale. The old farm house, falling down, instantly intrigued my husband. In its derelict state, it cried out for some love and attention. Excitedly, Michael saw possibility. Could we save and restore the old home?

Meanwhile, my eyes were transfixed on the mammoth oak tree standing only metres away. "I know you," I whispered under my breath. It was spring and the small regrowth was budding – symbolic of my own healing journey. I was at the beginning of a desperate need for a new life for my family and me.

It was the weekend before 11 September 2001 – a date etched in history, a time of grief-filled endings and beginnings.

Back then, as I looked up into the canopy of Oak, I instantly felt at home.

CHAPTER 1

Yesterday's Story

My hunch is correct. My young family and I move to the country a year after this. My path has brought me to a land that had witnessed the Gold Rush, the greed, the fortunes and great devastation. Hundreds had settled on this land with the promise of great wealth. Many didn't survive.

Now, my oak is the last one standing. Perhaps brought out from England in the pocket of a peasant, pushed into the earth with a wish and prayer. I'm sure she holds story, wisdom and a gift.

Connecting to her spirit now, I take three breaths, deep into my heart – my vortex language, no thought getting in the way.

"Hello."

I'm the first to speak. Then I wait in silence.

Unlike connections to other trees, I feel this oak is different. I take another three deep breaths. "Do you want to talk to me?"

I sense a stirring deep in Oak's core, but no words follow yet.

Holding her thick, rough bark, I feel her pain. Sadness wells in my open, connected heart. Without words, she shows me a picture of battle. Back in times of poverty, I see those who kill for scraps of food; for a small chunk – or flake – of gold.

I know she wants to take me back to her beginning. I see a primitive beginning – with people, mostly men, stealing from others as they sleep. Devoid of trust, living in makeshift shanties, 'survival' is the ultimate goal, not gold itself. Many die, victims of jealousy and greed.

"Why are you showing me this?" I interrupt the disturbing images of hardship, anger and despair.

She now speaks, for the first time, with a deep, mellow tone. "History tells yesterday's story. Unfortunately, it's a repeat cycle wearing another mask today, but with the same underlying lesson – one of jealousy, competition and greed."

"How is this relevant to me?"

I am excited that she's started speaking, and I hold curiosity for her gift, but I also feel a deep ache in my heart for the painful acts of human nature. I feel all the bloodshed she has witnessed.

"The relevance is in many countries, towns and cities. Worldwide, this is cracking and being pushed to the surface. Bigoted, racist, sexist, angry, terror-driven, greedy humans are going to kill the life in others. You, too, can be walking the earth, yet be dead."

She pauses.

"You know, a soul can suffocate years before their last breath is taken. Look into the eyes of those around you. So much sickness, lifelessness and emptiness. Fearing ridicule, judgement and exclusion, the human race has been dictated to. Forgetting their own essence, as if in a trance, they just go through the motions every day. They get out of bed but stay asleep through the day, until they return to bed, ready to repeat it all again the next day – and the next."

She pauses again. This time I cover my eyes as tears roll down my cheeks. I ask, "Do I need to encourage a wake-up?"

"You need to provide a new dream. In restful sleep, you need to plant seeds of possibility. Personal possibility for everyone – no two alike. It is time for you to wake to your own promise and encourage the same in others. Only then will people stop robbing, raping, controlling, dominating and hating each other. This is a reactive way of deflecting their own reflection. Wake people up to their purpose and a sense of self-love, then they won't want to hurt, kill or harm others."

She's beginning to make sense. Perhaps I wasn't ready for this message until now. "I am sad about the state of this world. I am ashamed to be human and guilty of not always supporting or providing a 'space' for others. I realise I was unable to do this when my own life felt so broken. Only when a sense of wholeness seeps through my own soul, can I then hold a supportive space for others without somehow feeling depleted myself."

My back feels her thick bark. I feel her support – yes. I also feel a sense of disquiet – the truth is uncomfortable.

"So what does the world need? Let me re-phrase that – what is your gift?"

"I'm going to thread a knowing and awareness. The gift I bring – you will discover. Please pen the journey. Sharing this is your gift – to give once you live and experience this miracle first-hand. A miracle is the alchemy magic of trust, action and living."

It sounds like a riddle. It also feels like a path on which I've been invited to walk.

CHAPTER 2

Death of the Soul

Now that our conversation has started, I'm curious about my new friend, Oak. Like a TV addict, I'm excited for the next episode.

Throwing on my tatty denim jeans and an old T-shirt, I casually walk over to my new friend. I cross my legs in a relaxed yoga style. I arrive with no poise, elegance or composure.

"Morning," I smile.

The leaves rustle 'hello' within her large canopy, one that spans at least 20 metres.

I take my three breaths, deep into my heart. "You left me intrigued when we last spoke. I couldn't wait to chat again. Is there anything you want to add about the gold rush times here?" Because our conversations are just beginning, I think that asking a question may continue the flow.

"Death is final – is it not?"

I'm a little shocked by Oak's directness. I nod.

"Birthing a baby back then was a chance of life or death."

She shows me images of a labouring woman. She is fair, delicate and weak. Holding her older three year old child's hand, I watch as the little boy is gripped with fear, seeing waves of contractions sweep over his mother. She is desperate to calm her son whilst also garnishing enough strength to bring her next baby into the world. Her fragile body trembles as contractions rock her to her core.

Then I see the young boy go stiff and begin convulsing – a shake that thrashes through his body. Mother and child are unable to help each other. Then silence ... nothing. The colour drains from both.

Slowly, the colour returns to the small boy's cheeks. He is confused, frightened and recovering from what appears to be an epileptic fit. Alone, he cries. His mother is dead. His unborn sister is also dead.

Seeing the images, loss, confusion and grief for the young boy, tears also soak my T-shirt. My heart aches. I take three more big breaths, trying to stay connected.

My friend Oak continues to tell the story.

"Anger then took this woman's husband captive. He was consumed with rage at everything and everyone in the world. A drought dried his tears. If his son cried, he was beaten. The son was labelled as 'Mad Dog' because his fits continued. Stones and curses were hurled at him. One day I witnessed his own father tying a noose around his neck and stringing him up in the pine tree that stood out the front of your home – the tree you recently cut down."

I knew about the pine tree's pain and how I felt around it. It had been dying for some time.

"Just a teenager, the boy hung and died in that tree. You see, evil twists a soul. Good or bad, souls are changed by tragedy. Anger consumed the boy's father. He found no peace – resulting in a hardened heart and a broken soul. Hurting others was easy because his heart was dead!"

My mind turns to my own brother at the ruthless hands of our father and the bullies at school, his life such a mess. He hurt, crushed and broke me. I'm confused why this parallel comes to me.

"What lesson is in this anger and pain?" I ask.

"So much pain. Stale, dead hearts stomp on the hearts of vulnerable, soft and open souls."

I hold my breath and then butt in. "I shut my own heart, in order to not feel my pain in front of others. I kept away from people who are full of hate. As a little girl I had no choice but to live with them, but when I grew I knew I needed to stay away from them. Aren't you making an excuse? Are you saying it's OK that this broken man back in Gold Rush times – and my own father and brother – just acted from pain and anger?"

As I say the words, I think I understand the lesson.

"Or are you just pointing out that it had nothing to do with the boy who lost his mother – or me as a young girl?"

"You are hearing the message. It is never the fault of one being hurt by such people. Those who hurt others are the problem."

"Yes, but many people want to 'fix' these people's anger by trying to 'love' them better. I watched my own mother making excuses for my brother. He just went on to hurt his own children and many others. What is the alternative?"

She shares more wisdom. "Only when the world turns away and stops making excuses, will those with stale, dead hearts realise they have a problem. Only when they want to heal and ask for help, will they change. If a tree is rotten, you chop it down. Yet people remain standing and continue to spread rot."

I question, "Just so I have it right, you need to clear out the people who hurt and harm others? We don't try to fix them unless they want to find healing? I guess jail bundles them together. I still think I'm missing something ..."

There is a long pause. I wonder if my friend Oak is frustrated at me not getting it straight up.

Then she says slowly, "I'm going to leave you with this. STOP pretending someone is good if they are not. No-one can change another unless they want to change. STOP pretending everything will be OK if you put up with it."

"Why are you telling me this?"

"Your brother is dead inside. Has been for years. Your mother has slowly died also, because she allows his evil – pretending he is really good. For everyone who allows and accepts an evil person to live with them – a father, mother, son, daughter, friend or partner – they invite death of their own soul. It is time to put stop to the fantasy. By inviting evil in, you eventually become the same on the inside."

I swallow. I am shocked by her bluntness. I think of all the people in powerful positions in the world – and the people who support them. Wow! Death of the soul!

I don't thank her. Instead, I place my hand on the earth that supports my oak. This message is more for the supporters. I too need to be mindful of the relationships I support. What do I allow space for in my life? How then does that feed or starve, and – in the end – maybe kill my soul?

CHAPTER 3

Holding Space

Walking up to Oak today, I want to reach out and touch her thick, rough and aged bark. I walk slowly around her trunk, over a metre in diameter. I don't feel like sitting today. I am still curious about our next conversation, but wonder if I need to brace myself after the last two encounters.

"Today I stand by you, rather than leaning on you. I face you, holding my arms up against you. Today I want to hold some 'space' for you, my friend. I acknowledge all the scenes that played out around you, etching into your soul, forever changing your view." I stand silently, looking towards the ground where her large legs are rooted firmly.

"Good morning, Rochelle." A gust of wind ruffles against me.

"Is it possible to share a beautiful moment today?

Something that brought love into view." Again, I wait in silence.

After a long pause, Oak responds: "There are many beautiful moments. Like the one I'm having right now. When someone stands, looks and takes in my beauty, it is a magical and happy moment. With honour, I witnessed kisses and affection between couples in love. Many moments of love. I want to share this with you."

I smile. I feel a shift in the energy all around me – a tingle, a freedom and a sense of belonging.

"Love is an energy. See, feel and hear love." She continues before showing me more images.

I see a picture of someone hearing the words, 'I love you', but still appearing alone and empty. Then I see swirls of colour engulfing a couple, with feelings so abundant and rich with love that no words are needed. Holding hands, a kiss, intimacy, standing facing each other with eyes and souls connecting. Scene after scene, I witness spaces that hold connections of love. Still smiling, inside I feel a lightness of being.

"Thank you."

I do not press, nor ask for more. I just continue to hold the space this morning. So far I'm glad I showed up.

"Everyone is usually in a hurry. Rushing suffocates love. When you're too busy, always thinking about, planning for tomorrow, when you hold expectations and justifications as your priority, you miss the love that is always around you, my friend. You have walked past me like a stranger for years. You have seen me but not acknowledged me. Only today, now, do I feel your love because you hold space for me without expectations. Thank you."

I feel guilty. I have always loved this tree. I would be devastated if anything happened to her. I always thought that just thinking that was enough. I lift my head from the ground, right up into the branches above.

"You are showing me what love really is," I say slowly. I think of all the times it has been too hard to show this love as I have battled my own feelings of being unloved and worthless. How I have longed for someone to just show up without any expectations, holding the space. I know I'm loved, I just don't feel it like this. Right now, I feel time is irrelevant. Nothing else matters but this transfixing moment.

The fine hairs on my skin stand on end, my head is light because it's not being drained anywhere else or jammed full of planning anything away from the here and now.

"This is such a beautiful gift, thank you."

Wow, imagine having moments of love in life with all I care about! Love for one of my boys by listening, showing up and holding the space – with no expectations, silencing my own mind.

I remember one of my fondest memories of being loved as a child. I was sitting with my mother's father. We talked as Granddad held the space, and I felt the love. I know there is a massive difference when Michael and I unite without expectation, spontaneously showing love for one another. This needs to happen more often.

"Love is the gift of presence. Thank you for holding your hands to my bark and holding a space today," Oak whispers.

Today my lesson, my gift, is love.

CHAPTER 4

Birds' Balance

The sun has cast its scorching beams, drying and hardening the ground. This morning as I open my curtain, looking down on Oak, I see rain – so much rain that the pathways are now running streams. The dam is bursting its embankment to join nearby creeks. The air is fresh as I carefully make my way across to Oak. I tread with caution to avoid ending up in the mud. I remain standing.

"Standing the test of time, I bet you have witnessed many downpours and floods." Without even saying hello, I have opened the conversation. Then I say politely, "Oh, sorry. Good morning Oak. How are you this morning?"

Large drops soak my clothing. Within moments I feel chilled and decide to remove my outer layer to sit on, after all. I curl up so my body can feel protected.

"I feel rejuvenated this morning. The thirst of Mother Earth has been quenched. Thank you for asking."

Pulling myself into a tighter ball, I sit in silence for a little while. Oak has not continued speaking or showing me scenes from yesterday. I sit and wait. As I do, I hear a bird chorus, a happy tune that instantly brings a smile to my face. We have an abundance of birds here. Often, I stumble across a discarded nest. Different in design and style, they are kept in my art room or around the house. A symbol of home itself as they were once a haven for a mother, eggs and babies.

I have always loved all things bird-related: the time taken to weave a new nest for their young. I have nests made from fine twigs, part of branches with leaves still attached. Some dog fur is in the centre of one, and some are open like a bowl, or completely closed but for a small opening.

As a little girl, feathers were my gift. I would always notice a feather's colour, shape and size. I just picked them up and noticed how I felt, bringing the treasures home. When we first moved to the farm, Michael would bring birds that had been hit by the side of the road. My art room also holds the preserved wings. Yes, I love birds!

"Oak, is there anything you can tell me about the birds here?" A gust of wind brings a heavy shower, soaking me right through.

"Grace, ease, strength, determination, soulful song, scratching, flapping, feeding, community, solitude, souring, hiding, waiting ... birds are the gifted that settle on earth, yet live in the air. This is why anything you treasure from a bird is a gift. Birds are the only animal that both fly and walk."

It makes sense. I have never thought about it that much.

"You, my friend, are like the bird. You live on earth, yet connect to beyond." I'd never thought of this before either.

I quietly wait for more, not wanting to interrupt the simplicity of what Oak is telling me. Or is the message deeper?

"Too many people only walk the earth. They never live beyond, they don't dream. A dream is never where you are. In a dream, you are always taken to another time and place. Dreaming is a place of learning, freedom and balance. It is how you can connect back to a happy event and re-live the joy. Also, it connects you into an event full of fear. If you go there, you re-live it."

I am now sitting up and listening carefully. Like in a silent movie, Oak shows me what she means.

I watch as I am taken to a time of great fear in my childhood. I am restrained and my father is breaking open my soul. My body is as stiff as a corpse, my soul escaping as I shut down.

"Why are you taking me here?" A single tear makes its way down my cheek. As an adult, I connect to the pain of my little girl.

"Sshh, keep on watching."

As I shut out the horror as a little girl, I float downstairs to play in a dreaming spirit world. I am free, happy and laughing. Such a contrast to the events taking place upstairs at the hands of the monster. Eventually back in my body and tucked in bed, I seem unaffected. The following day goes on as usual. I'm OK.

The screen goes blank and then I see my son being rushed over the hill at the farm because of an accident on his motorbike. His shoulder is dislocated.

He is not screaming, but calm. Strangely I am, also. I know the drill. I call Emergency and pack a bag. It's calm and slow and eventually he is lying on a hospital bed with his shoulder back where it should be. Oh sure, my son is pumped full of drugs so they can wrench everything back into place. But what I see is order.

The screen changes to another time. I am giving birth. Focussing on a corner in the room I have the power to completely numb out. My mind and body are unaware of the pain as new life enters.

I sit a little confused, cold and wet. Confusion is becoming common for me with my friend.

"Alright, I see the contrast between being completely present and then numbing to shield pain, a horrible event or accident. Is this the contrast with land and air in birds?"

"If you watch a bird glide, they are not stressed. Only on land do they forage for food or frantically build nests for their family. Extremes of this shown in your own life. In everyday life you are doing. Earth is busy and at times hectic. You rest only when you sleep, and you meditate to relax and give your mind and body space. Flying like a bird – numbing out – is about 'balance' and survival. Your survival called on you often."

There is a pause before Oak continues: "Why do you think people are addicted to drugs, alcohol or food? It is a way of numbing out. There is desperation for balance when people cannot relax, dream or meditate — taking a walk, run, going to the gym, yoga or anything that allows stillness of the mind. You, my friend, need balance. You are unable to disconnect anymore by numbing out, so you need to create space daily to regain your balance."

It all makes sense. I know all too well how scattered I become if there is no space, dreaming or break from the earthly world in which I live.

"Balance — living on earth and the important freedom of flying," are her final words today.

Shivering, I smile and touch her trunk. Then I make a dash for the back door. As we have chatted today, the waters have risen.

CHAPTER 5

Support

With the earth waterlogged and spongy underfoot, I feel I could easily be swallowed. There's been more rain in the last 24 hours than would usually fall in a month. Oak's branches are heavy. Her canopy's massive fingertips nearly touch the ground.

"Morning," I make my way over and duck under her green foliage.

"Extremes. No longer thirsty, but drowning." Oak wastes no time in responding today. She has been waiting for me.

"Are you OK?" I look up as water splashes onto my face.

"My stability has taken years. I have withstood flood, strong wind and even fire. My roots are as large as my canopy and beyond."

I look out beyond Oak and imagine her massive network underground. She is held and supported. "Wow, that's pretty incredible. Do you communicate with one another?" I point to the other trees.

"Oh yes, we are a community. The space always changes for all of us, when another tree falls."

I am transported to our city home. A large tree was cut down just outside our front door. I was told it was sick and needed to go. A couple of years later, I still feel its loss. I cannot imagine what nature itself feels when death visits.

"Loss is different for everyone. Life's cycle of beginnings and endings. Each generation is seeded by the previous one. Notice if you cut a tree down, soon baby offshoots are growing everywhere. Life continues."

I consider how the tree is symbolic of people. If we are supported by good communities and networks we can endure extreme situations. I instantly think of various groups of which I've been a part – like-minded people supporting each another. These days with social media, it is easy to connect superficially. At times, however, I haven't always felt connection, support and community. I have struggled more without this when problems have arisen in my life.

"Are you telling me I need community?"

"Not just any community – you need your tribe."

I smile and know what Oak means. I don't always feel understood; in fact, I often felt misunderstood as I grew. Now I just move toward people until it fits. All of a sudden, I'm wrenched with sadness. At the start of the year, I faced a part of my life full of deep agony. My raw, painful childhood was ripped open in a courtroom. I had amazing support from Michael and the boys but my extended family struggled with my confronting situation. I found, at the time, the lack of support was like being abused all over again. I felt I didn't matter. It was a dark time, and I struggled deeply. Without anyone at all by my side, I'm sure I would have fallen over. The biggest storms can be endured, provided you have support.

My thoughts go to Senegal Africa where I will travel with *The Hunger Project* in a couple of months. *The Hunger Project*'s philosophy is to create community and support. When this happens, hardship can be endured. Without it, there is devastation.

"I pledge to you today, Oak, to stand up and support humanity. I also pledge to find my tribe worldwide – united, we will all do great things."

"Trees are global too," Oak interrupts my thoughts. "Underground is our network. It is our strength and survival."

Holding my hand on an exposed root, I envisage the network for both humans and nature alike.

CHAPTER 6

Reflections

It's evening and the rain has stopped. Now what I hear is the flow and rush of water in the nearby creek as it pours into the massive dam beside Oak. Music resounds – the songs of the ducks, cockies and the many birds as they explode into concert. I sit on a large root at the back of Oak, my back reclining with ease in the perfect angle of her trunk.

Taking my three breaths into my heart, I open the channel of love and communication.

"You are very beautiful at dusk," I say, looking up and around at the softness enveloping Oak.

"Real beauty is beyond your vision. How do you feel around beauty?" my friend asks.

"Well, it's interesting, because in your beauty I see my own." I'm proud of my honesty here.

"If you saw me as ugly, your experience would be your own ugly truths," Oak adds.

I let her words sink in. I think of all the times I've noticed something or someone being grotesque. Indeed, I too have felt ugly and not beautiful in comparison.

I see magazine pages filled with images of beautiful people. Instantly, I want to have what makes them beautiful. A magnet pulls me toward beauty.

"There is enormous power in what you see, how that makes you feel and then how it connects into that speck of who you are. All aspects you see are within you. The ugly, beauty, angry, happy, calm, anxious – every single facet is present within you."

Silence enables her meaning to settle.

"The awareness of this is priceless – thank you." I am grateful that right now, in this moment, the soft hue of sunset casts the silhouettes of the native gums over the dam water. The frogs have joined the musical chorus. The music softens and almost lulls me to sleep. I could be inside right now, watching television, taken somewhere so different. How my reflection is being experienced is my choice.

After some time, my trance-like state is interrupted.

"Conflict is part of life. Be careful what you drag in as yours. Never give your beauty to an ugly scene."

Oak's words are so loving. My environment, a gift. The simplicity is beautiful – and so am I if I honour myself enough with a space that supports me.

The sun has just about dipped her head. It's a full moon here tonight, a time when I love to manifest my wishes. My dream right now is the view that draws me closer to a beautiful 'me'.

"Good night, Oak. I hope your wishes and dreams are abundant."

I don't want to leave. So I stay until the moon replaces the sun fully.

CHAPTER 7

Togetherness

It's a nice view this morning as I make my way towards Oak. In my mind's eye I see a vision of a table being set up. A meal is spread, ready for the 'togetherness' about to be celebrated. As the scene flashes to a past time, I even see my own young family, having just arrived to our new life in the country. Our favourite spot was always under the massive canopy of Oak.

Making myself comfortable, the mood for today is already set. It's a fun, happy mood, full of love.

"Togetherness," I say.

"Celebration," Oak's chorus echoes back at me. "The ultimate gift in life is sharing a moment over food with others."

The vision continues, showing me all the generations before me. Rugs are laid out, people sit and eat together. Picnics and feasts. Simple and elaborate. Many parties with cakes and candles. Older people with cakes bursting with candles, and young children with just precious few candles. *Happy Birthday* sung, over and over. I also witness Easter egg hunts, Christmas celebrations, engagements and weddings. Many, many moments of love.

"Wow, you have witnessed so many moments of togetherness, right here," I say, stating the obvious. "My favourite pastime is always coupled with food, feeding the people I love."

"I was sad when you stopped celebrating under my branches, once your home was built. You should come back and set up under here," she invites me. Oak is right. No building matches the feel of this place.

"I have loved these moments as much as you. As much as you like cooking and feeding, I love sheltering you all."

"Togetherness," I repeat. "I have a birthday party at the farm next weekend. I promise to invite you. My friend, sharing cake under you will be special." Images of family, young and old, under my outside room ... perfect. A picnic, it will be. My menu plans are beginning.

"Thank you for sharing the vision this morning. Please manifest good weather for me." I already know the forecast for the following weeks include showers.

I sit and rest at my favourite spot around Oak. Like an armchair, she supports and comforts me. I'm in no hurry this morning. I am bursting with happiness from all the parties I have witnessed. I imagine my friend Oak with balloons hanging from her limbs and brightly-coloured cake, fairy bread and party finger food.

CHAPTER 8

Self-Sabotage

This morning as I wake, my own issue of self-sabotage plays in my mind. This is my weakness, a method and way of numbing out.

About four months ago I pledged not to drink alcohol and instead only eat food that supported a slimmer, healthier me. On a few occasions, at party celebrations, I said 'to hell with it', drank up and broke my pledge to myself. Before I knew it, all my promises were then broken. I ended up bingeing for a week beyond each celebration. This was my cycle, a trap that undid my hard work.

This morning as I visit my friend Oak, I have a specific question about my trap of self-sabotage and the repeated self-loathing that consumes me.

"Morning Oak," I say, dejected. "Why does my lack of self-love and honour undo all my hard work?

As soon as I give up my promise of not drinking or binge-eating, my self-loathing escalates for days."

My belly still full from yesterday, I feel sick in my mind, body and spirit. They are filled with self-hate right now.

"Good morning, Rochelle. I see your void. At the bottom of this deep, dark vacuum, you have a feeling in the pit of self. Pity stems from this place. Before you knew of alcohol and binge-eating you already knew this feeling. As a little girl you sat in this same putrid place."

I hang my head in shame and sadness.

"This has been programmed within your being. You were taught that you weren't worth loving. Events reinforced that feeling. Whenever you feel happy and healthy, these old feelings are triggered within you."

Unfortunately, I know all of this to be so true. What I don't know is how to stop it. "Can you help me?" Although I'm not on my knees pleading, I feel as though I am. My own sense of uselessness is swallowing me in big gulps of despair.

Oak begins to shed her light. "Let's go back to

the beginning. There is a short circuit inside you that needs re-wiring."

I think of all the times I've worked on this problem, all the professionals I have consulted, my learning and intelligence on which I have tried to draw.

"You learned to be your own monster – programmed to deserve only pain, self-loathing and self-defeat."

"Yes I know," I nod. I feel I've failed. "I want to scream at that part within me that continues this pain," I confess.

"I see your battle. Just like the fights I saw over gold. In the end, one always died before the other won the gold."

"I know the battle. Is there a part in me that has to die?" I ask.

"Yes – you are dying anyway. Who do you want to win the battle?" Her blunt, harsh truth cuts through me.

I reply, "The healthy, happy me, of course."

"The evil corpse inside of you needs to be killed

and no longer given breath. Remember when we spoke of stone hearts? By remaining around such sources of death, you also lose your love."

I nod.

"Rest your back against me. Close your eyes. Inside, see all the darkness and all the light. The light is all the good thoughts, feelings and love. The dark is like sharp knives, being gagged and every single feeling, word and event that accumulated in you to become evil – to 'live' backwards. As soon as you shine light in darkness, the darkness vanishes. Keeping your eyes closed – watch what happens."

I watch as the tangled, knotted events of hatred are wrenched out like weeds. I watch foul-smelling sludge being removed, bucket by bucket. The stench of vomit-like odour is washed, scrubbed, removed. My internal dialogue is rewound, and tape after tape of recording is removed. Self-loathing words are pulled like streamers from each cassette. Then I collect the piles of mess and dump them into large garbage bags.

I watch what looks like the home of a hoarder being cleaned. So much mess, old useless memory and filth. I see the shell of my home, myself. Everything is taken out. Perhaps a will be renovation possible once the rubbish is removed. In the end, the house is pushed over. My own Ground Zero. Rubble, even death. My own ending.

We have gone right back. I'm now seeing the beginning of Oak – an acorn being planted, watered by rain and warmed by sun. From a tiny seedling I watch through time-lapsed images until I see the massive tree Oak, as she stands today, for just a moment.

I feel calm. My pain and my self-abuse darkness are now lightened, replaced by new growth.

"Thank you ... I think!" I honestly confess. I am interested to see if there is a shift.

"Remember not to invite or be around stone hearts. Always dine and live with what feeds love in your soul."

I rest in Oak's words. I lay my exhausted body down and sleep, right by Oak. My dreaming takes me to a space that I hold lovingly for myself, just as I held space the other day for Oak. The test comes in the dreaming space when I see an extended gathering. I share something personal and am immediately mocked. I feel sad and misunderstood.

"Oak, am I being shown to be careful about who I let in close and share myself with?" I ask her for further guidance.

"It is exactly what you need to remember. Trust must always be built and earned. If you are broken by someone, never go back to this same person expecting a different result."

I see the faces in my dream and am grateful for its warning. "Thank you. I too often try to win people over who aren't always meant to be that close."

Now that Oak has cleared out to replace with new beginnings, I need to treat myself with self-love, protection and nurture. I am hoping to return to my pledge of clean, healthy habits.

I feel drained as I get up from beside Oak. I hold my hand on a tiny new green shoot on her aged thick trunk. Newness is always possible. I wrap my arms around myself.

Today is a new day.

CHAPTER 9

War's Battle Never Won

Before sitting at Oak's feet today, I need to walk up over my hill. My head is jam-packed and bursting with distractions. The air is fragrant and cool. "Isn't this meant to be summer?" I ask myself as the climb gets steeper. As my body awakens, it encourages my mind to still and relax. I walk for about half an hour before I make my way back down my hill. I enjoy seeing Oak's large presence come into view.

"Morning Oak." I sit in her comfort, my armchair made of her root base and reclining bark trunk. "Argh," I let out a sigh as I slump into Oak's support.

"I've been waiting to see how you feel today," Oak checks in with me. "Have you felt the shift?"

From head to toe, I check how I feel. "Other than my awkward, active mind first thing this morning, with my thoughts darting all over the place with ideas, I feel pretty good," I confess. "I didn't wake up as usual, obsessing over food without even really being hungry. I know this is how I try to numb out. The clean-out you helped me with yesterday has allowed a sense of balance. Thank you."

"Now that you are comfortable, I'd like to show you something." Closing my eyes, I witness many families gathering around this very area of Oak. Down by the dam they also spread out under the surrounding gums. Dressed in old-fashioned clothing, I notice girls in their long dresses and boys wearing caps. In a time-warped journey I'm taken back to what looks like a country fair. There are sack-races and apples in a barrel of water, each person taking it in turn to retrieve an apple with only their mouths. There's a game made with sticks in the ground, with hoops of bendy twigs then thrown over the sticks. I have seen modern-day replicas of these games. I smile. Prizes of cake or candy are given to the winners.

Then I'm shown some of the boys from this carefree scene now dressed as soldiers. The war has begun. The boys are excited, while their families' faces display worry and despair. I see women crying, wondering if they will ever see their sons again. The men put on a brave front as they act proud and encouraging for their sons.

Oak interrupts: "No son returned the same. Some didn't return at all. Another notch in history's belt. A time of great loss. Even those who returned were forever changed. Souls broken on battlefields. Dead – yes, something died within."

I contrast Oak's words with the visions of the country fair.

"When war was over, what did the world feel like back then?" I ask quietly, knowing I'll always get truth from Oak.

"A darkness cast doom and gloom. The mask of worry was worn throughout town. People stopped meeting here in celebration for a very long time. I felt the world's pain above and beneath me. More endings than beginnings." Oak becomes silent.

I feel her sadness and emptiness as she thinks about this time. I try to imagine: what would it be like to feel loss, so much loss? "How did the world recover? What happened in the years after the war?" I try to shift to a possible better time.

Closing my eyes again, I'm shown soldiers exploding like time-bombs, triggered from the battlefield. They explode with anger at being so misunderstood by a community that hasn't witnessed the frontline. Some soldiers take their own lives after arriving back home. They are pushed to the limit. More time passes as I'm shown a few who were once boys, now men working the land. Tending livestock has become their new pastime. Some fall in love and marry, then have children of their own. Generations of farmers now work the land around Oak.

"You have been witness to so much hardship," I say, with love.

"Yes, my friend, this is a good example of polarity between human experiences. There are extreme emotional shifts between joy and sorrow, one's own light and dark sides, between one's humanity and spirit." Oak rustles her leaves. It almost seems like it all makes her shiver. Or is she trying to shake off the past?

"Thank you for sharing this part of your history with me. I know some of your chapters have been full of pain."

In polite respect for Oak's obvious grave mood, I decide to just leave our conversation there. Holding my hands on the earth, I invoke her support. I gently stand and walk away; new images in my heart and mind.

CHAPTER 10

Oak's Gift

Waking early before sunrise, I feel stillness outside calling to me. With just enough light to see, I decide to sit with Oak. Touching my hand gently to her, I whisper, "Morning, my friend. You feel like a grandmother to me, not just a friend. I would love to call you by name."

"Thank you for asking. My name is Agnes, which means 'pure'," Oak warmly answers.

"I feel very fortunate to have such an old spirit who lives up to her name. I feel humbled to be living beside you here at our farm," I whisper.

"I loved the day your young family made this place home," Agnes responds.

My memory takes me back to the time we drove up to the original farm gate, unopened for about 20 years. I see the old farmhouse, once two separate relocated houses, sitting beside each other, joined only by the verandahs. I smile as I remember the bunches of daffodils the boys gathered to gift to me. This was the first time I recognised Oak. I know now, this wasn't the first time I saw her. Back then, I had no idea the impact Agnes would have on my life.

Oak's heart speaks. "Your boys brought new energy. New stories of adventure, courage and love. Somersaults on trampolines and even into the dam. They built makeshift cubby houses. I'm always amused at the contraptions towed behind something, anything with a motor. Your boys have gifted a beautiful spirit here. I loved it when they would swing from my braches. I felt that I held them in my arms. Occasionally they would turn and look at me, and you and Michael did the same. It made me proud to be part of the plans of your family home. I hear you talk of my importance. My spirit thanks you."

The sun lights the sky. The songs of frogs and solo birds echo across the land.

I acknowledge Agnes's words and hold the gratitude. She continues, "Please share the gift of my dreaming and essence with others."

"The other day when you let me pick some of

your branches to take inside the house, I kept a little of you. Intuitively, in alchemy style, I have bottled you up, so your essence can be experienced by all," I excitedly tell Agnes.

"When I use this alchemy oil, I feel your spirit tingle on my skin. I feel truth and honesty. Removing my mask, I feel 'me'. This oil holds the energy of the day I saw your beauty, and then my own. Your raw honesty gives me comfort. It's a real change to my life in so many ways. For a long time, I worried about my façade, hiding my real truth. You, my friend, hide nothing. I trust you — and because of this, I trust myself. Good is good and bad is bad. You taught me to wake up, be real and only allow heart closeness with those who deserve it." I hold my hands on Agnes's trunk and instantly feel the firm love of Grandmother Oak.

"You are seeded with my soul. Please seed others with my love," Agnes asks me.

I know that if a tree gifts wisdom or dreaming, it is never just for me. I close my eyes, still holding onto Grandmother Agnes. I feel her pure love, protection and truth.

"Gratitude ... I have so much gratitude for your wisdom. In dreams, you gave me your gift. I feel your love. Thank you."

I drop my hands to my sides. Sitting in my comfortable seat at her base I feel supported.

I rest, feel, remember, love, honour all – in the space of 'me'.

CHAPTER 11

Celebration

I gather blown-up multi-coloured balloons into bunches and tie them to the outer tips of my beautiful Oak Agnes. Today she is invited to our party. Out under her shaded canopy, I have set up long tables covered in brightly-coloured cloth, ready for our feast. Over twenty chairs are scattered around in a circle. Instantly I feel Agnes Oak's joy and happiness.

"Today you are Grandmother at my gathering," I smile up at Oak. Our guests today are family. Being under her shade reminds me of all the times we ate here before our home was built. As soon as Ali sees where the tables are set up under Oak, she begins searching for old photos of gatherings when my boys were young.

After the main barbeque lunch is served we tie piñatas filled with lollies to Oak's larger branches.

Each person, from youngest to oldest, plays the game. They are blindfolded and take turns to hit the piñatas with a stick and free the goodies inside. Chocolates and lollies fly everywhere and the kids gather in excitement. It is fun. *Happy Birthday* is sung and candles are blown out. Today is special.

During the afternoon I notice beautiful moments where space is held for each other. It has been a little while since I have held a real feeling of family in such a way. During the party, I notice everyone commenting on Oak's beauty.

"Have you enjoyed the party?" I ask Oak when the party is finished and as I begin packing everything away, before the sun sets.

"My heart is bursting today. Thank you for inviting me, for allowing my arms to shade and love you." Even though there is no breeze, Oak gives a rustle. "I heard all the beautiful comments of love and admiration as the guests looked up. Thank you." As Grandmother Agnes Oak speaks, I also hear birds sing out in chorus together.

"Home is where the heart is, and your heart is seeded inside mine. The grandmother I always wanted, I have found in you. Your kind, direct guidance has certainly set me thinking differently. I feel my own life enriched now, with new boundaries."

Sitting on my favourite tree armchair at her base, I rest in her support, strength and love. The view of the Australian countryside is breathtaking. A family of ducks swims in the nearby water. I don't always feel such a sense of belonging, but today I do.

"Space for you today," I smile, touching my hand to my heart. "Space also for me."

Agnes Oak speaks slowly. "Share the importance of creating what you crave. Never sit sad, waiting for it to all just happen. Embrace moments. This is the lesson, the gift. To embrace completely those who can mirror, reflect, your own heart."

Both of my hands are on my heart. Closing my eyes, I hear quiet. Breaking the silence, I say, "Thank you for seeding me your wisdom, reflection and heart. I promise to continue showing up and holding space. I love you."

I feel her love tingle in my own limbs, in my body and mind. Circles of engulfing colour swirl around us both. My back is still supported by her trunk.

"Thank you for taking and penning our journey. I love you too."

I don't want to break this magic bubble, so I take my time. With hands now in a position of prayer in front of my heart, I whisper to the universe, "thank you, thank you, thank you ..."

It is not by chance that I am gifted by the grand, wise Oak Agnes.

Also by Rochelle

Banyan Tree Wisdom: My Gift to You

Banyan Tree Wisdom: Wisdom Cards

Meeting Rosie Banyan:
Learning Forgiveness, Trust and Love

I Give You My Word: Journal

EARTH GIANT TREE GIFT SERIES (GIFT BOOKS & AUDIO BOOKS)

Book 1: Oak Tree's Gift

Book 2: Baobab Tree's Gift

Book 3: Banyan Tree's Gift

Book 4: Rainbow Gum's Gift

ALCHEMY OILS

Banyan Tree: 'Restore Balance', 'Dream',
'Release' & 'Beauty Wisdom Power'

Oak Tree: 'Truth'

Baobab Tree 'Connection'

Banyan Tree 'Balance'

Rainbow Gum 'Joy'

www.treevoice.global

About the Author

A busy business owner, wife and mother, Rochelle thrived in the corporate and finance world in her early adult years. Then, after her fourth son, a wave of post-natal depression debilitated her, forcing her to re-visit the horrors of her sexually abusive childhood. With grit and determination she laboured against her own broken past and breathed life back into her shutdown heart, cracking open its language and capturing it in writing. She learned to trust in the universal soul path she'd stepped onto.

Each time she experienced a healing method that helped her, Rochelle became qualified in that field to then help others. She became a Bowen Therapist, Reiki and Seichem Master, Clinical Hypnotherapist using NLP methods, Journey Worker and Intuitive Healer. She also owned and ran a Day Spa and Healing Centre in North East Victoria.

Rochelle now immerses herself in connections with nature as they flow, bringing to life the lessons and messages through writing, speaking and facilitating. Her journey has led her to many parts of the globe. She has pitched to Hollywood in New York; she has hosted women's retreats in Bali; she has learned from poverty-stricken leaders in Senegal Africa; and she has discovered the 'simple' life in Vanuatu.

Rochelle's message is honest, raw and authentic, and her words are greatly needed as we all navigate our next chapter here on earth.

**AUTHOR, SPEAKER, ALCHEMIST,
A LOVER OF NATURE AND
VIBRANT LIVING**

Connect with Rochelle

hello@treevoice.global

business.facebook.com/TreeVoiceAuthor

www.facebook.com/RochelleHeverenAuthor

Instagram: @rochelle_with_love_x

www.treevoice.global

www.ingramcontent.com/pod-product-compliance
Lightning Source LLC
Chambersburg PA
CBHW032051290426
44110CB00012B/1045